psyched for science

Super Science Projects About Oceans

Allan B. Cobb

the rosen publishing group's
rosen central
new york

To my mom and dad for always encouraging my love of science and nature.

Published in 2000 by The Rosen Publishing Group, Inc.
29 East 21st Street, New York, NY 10010

First Edition

Library of Congress Cataloging-in-Publication Data

Cobb, Allan B.
        Super science projects about oceans / Allan B. Cobb.
            p. cm. — (Psyched for science)
        Includes bibliographical references and index.
        Summary: Presents science projects that demonstrate facts about oceans, including the water cycle, buoyancy, density, pressure, depth, waves, and tides.
        ISBN 0-8239-3174-9 (lib. bdg.)
        1. Oceanography—Experiments—Juvenile literature. 2. Science projects—Juvenile literature. [1. Oceanography—Experiments. 2. Experiments. 3. Science projects.] I. Title. II. Series.
GC21.5 .C63   2000
551.46'0078—dc21

                                                                                        99-044867

Manufactured in the United States of America

contents

Introduction

All About Oceans

If you look at a globe, you will see that most of the earth's surface is covered by water. In fact, more than 70 percent of the earth's surface is water. About 97 percent of this water can be found in the oceans. Water is the most common substance on our planet. Because of this, Earth is often referred to as the water planet.

Water is very important to life on earth. Every organism, or living thing, depends on water to survive. Did you know that the body of an adult man contains about nineteen quarts, or nineteen liters, of water? Human beings are about 65 percent water. Without water you would die.

This book concentrates on some of the physical properties of water and the oceans. It covers six different areas: the water cycle, buoyancy, density, pressure, waves, and tides.

All of the water on earth passes through the oceans as part of the water cycle. The water cycle

is the path that water follows as it travels between sea, air, and land. You will learn about the water cycle by building a working model of it.

Two of water's most important properties are buoyancy and density. Buoyancy is the upward force that water exerts on objects. It is what makes an object sink or float. Density is the weight of a given volume of water. Depending on the temperature and the salt content of the water, the density can change. The ocean has currents because of density differences.

If you want to understand the ocean, you will also need to know about pressure. Pressure is the force water makes as it presses down on an object. As water gets deeper, it creates more pressure. Pressure is very important to scuba divers, who swim deep in the ocean.

Just as all oceans have waves, they all have tides, too. Tides are the regular changes in sea level. Do you understand what causes waves and tides? Do you know how they work? This book will help you answer those questions.

The experiments in this book provide detailed instructions for getting started in your study of oceans. Beyond that, they depend on your observations. Each activity has its own instructions and safety warnings. Read on to discover more about oceans.

1 The Water Cycle

From the age of the dinosaur to the space age, the earth has always had and always will have exactly the same amount of water. Water is not created or destroyed; it simply changes from one form to another. It is used and reused over and over but is never used up. Every time you brush your teeth, you are using water that has existed for millions of years.

The water cycle explains the way that water moves between the ocean, air, and land. It is sometimes called the hydrologic cycle. The basic steps in the water cycle are evaporation, condensation, and precipitation. Evaporation occurs when water is heated and becomes a gas. The sun's heat evaporates ocean water, and the water goes into the air. When it cools, it condenses, or turns back into a liquid. Then the water falls as precipitation: rain, sleet, snow, or hail. Most of the precipitation falls back into the oceans. The rest falls onto the land, where it soaks into the ground; runs off into streams, rivers, or lakes; or

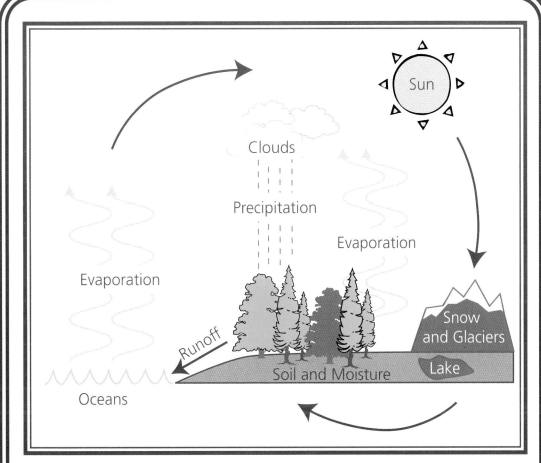

The Water Cycle

evaporates. The water that flows through the streams, rivers, and lakes eventually makes it back to the ocean. Then the entire cycle begins again.

Experiment #1

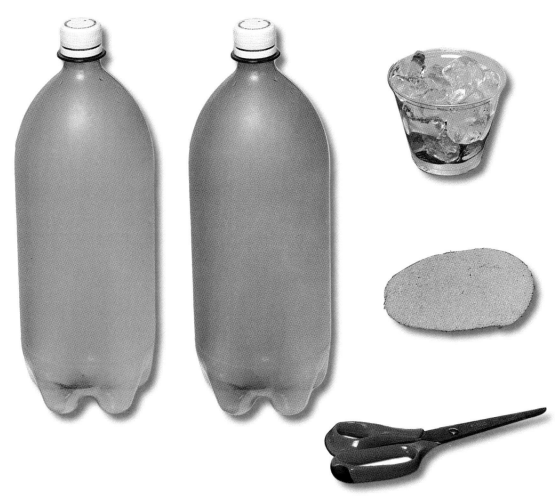

- Two 2-liter plastic soft-drink bottles
- Sand
- Scissors
- Water
- Ice cubes

The Water Cycle

What You'll Do

#1 Place the two plastic soft-drink bottles on their sides. Cut off the top of one bottle, and cut off the bottom of the other bottle.

#2 Fill the topless bottle with sand to a depth of about 4 inches (10 cm).

#3 Pour water into the bottle. The water should disappear into the sand. It won't remain separate or float on top of it.

Experiment #1

What You'll Do

#4 Place the bottom from the other bottle on top of the topless bottle. Place the ice cubes in the bottom of the upper bottle.

#5 Place the bottles near a strong lamp or in direct sunlight.

Analyzing Your Results

#1 Why did you put the bottles near a strong lamp or in direct sunlight?

#2 Where did the water that formed on the topless bottle come from?

#3 Draw a diagram of both bottles together. Identify what kind of cycle the water is following.

#4 If most of the water in the water cycle evaporates from the oceans, why don't the oceans become saltier?

For Further Investigation

#1 Think of a way to increase the amount of water that moves through your demonstration of the water cycle.

#2 Construction causes the surface of our land to change. One of its changes is to make impervious cover. Impervious cover is anything that covers the ground and prevents water from passing either into or out of it. Paved roads, houses, driveways, and parking lots are examples of impervious cover. Use plastic wrap to represent impervious cover in your model. How does impervious cover affect your model?

2 Sink or Float?

Have you ever wondered why some objects float whereas others sink? It will probably surprise you to know that an object's weight is only one part of the puzzle. A one-pound stick will float, but a one-pound rock will sink. Why?

For an object to float, it must weigh less than an equal volume of water. Volume is the amount of space that an object takes up. For example, a shoe box filled with air and a shoe box filled with sand have the same volume. They take up the same amount of space. However, they have different weights, since sand is much heavier than air.

What does this have to do with water and flotation? Well, when you put an object in water, you displace (or move) a volume of water that equals the object's volume. Basically, two things cannot take up the same space, so one of them has to move. If the object weighs more than the water, it sinks and pushes the water out of its way. If the water weighs more than the object, the object will float because the water will not allow itself to be moved aside. The upward force of the water that causes an object to float is called buoyancy.

You may have heard that it is easier to float in the ocean than in a lake. That is because oceans are saltwater, and most lakes are freshwater. When salt dissolves in water, it actually increases the weight of the water. Because the water now weighs more, it exerts a greater buoyant force.

In this activity, you will explore how adding salt to water increases the buoyant force. After this activity, you will be able to decide which of the earth's bodies of water it is easiest to float in—a lake, an ocean, or perhaps even some-where else.

Experiment #2

What You Need

- A large jar (1 quart, 1 liter, or larger)
- Water
- A pen cap
- Modeling clay
- A tablespoon
- Table salt

Sink or Float?

What You'll Do

#1 Fill the jar three-quarters full with water.

#2 Place the pen cap in the jar. Does it sink or float?

#3 Remove the pen cap from the jar. Place a small amount of modeling clay in the cap and put it back in the jar. Continue doing this until the pen cap begins to sink when placed in the jar. If it sinks quickly, remove a small amount of the modeling clay.

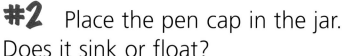

15

#4 Add one tablespoon of table salt to the water. Stir the water with the spoon until the salt dissolves. Is there any change in the

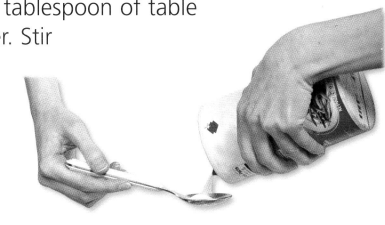

position of the pen cap?

#5 Add another table-spoon of table salt to the water. Again stir until the salt dissolves. Did the position of the pen cap change once more?

#6 Continue adding table salt and stirring. Do this three more times. Observe the position of the pen cap after adding each tablespoon of salt.

Sink or Float?

Analyzing Your Results

#1 How did the position of the pen cap change as you added salt to the jar?

#2 Given what you have just seen, do you think it would be possible for a log to sink in freshwater but float in salt water?

#3 Ships routinely travel from the Atlantic Ocean to ports on the Great Lakes. The Great Lakes are freshwater.

Great Salt Lake

What problems might a ship encounter when traveling from the Atlantic Ocean to the Great Lakes? What problems might a ship encounter when traveling from the Great Lakes to the Atlantic Ocean?

Great Salt Lake in Utah is the remains of a much older body of water. Because most of the water has evaporated, it is very salty. Do you think it is easier to float in Great Salt Lake than in other lakes?

For Further Investigation

Put a plastic film canister in the jar. Does it sink or float? Add sand to make the film canister heavier. Can you make it stay suspended in the water so that it neither sinks nor floats? How?

3 Water Density

You have proved that water exerts a buoyant force that causes objects to float or sink. But buoyancy can do far more than just this. This same buoyant force can keep bodies of water apart. How does it do this? It all depends on weight; not all water weighs the same amount. One body of water can be lighter or heavier than another. Density is the weight of a given volume of water and is an important property of water.

Remember when you learned about the water cycle? Water changes from a liquid to a gas when it evaporates. It then changes back to a liquid when it condenses. The same volume of water weighs more when it is a liquid than a gas. Water in its liquid state has a greater density than water in its gaseous state.

Why? When water changes temperature, it either expands (gets bigger) or contracts (gets smaller). When water gets warmer, its molecules move more quickly. Molecules are tiny particles that make up all matter. The molecules bounce around, taking up more space, and the water expands. When water gets cooler, its molecules move more slowly. They move closer together, taking up less space, and the water contracts. You see, the temperature of water affects the speed of the molecules, and that determines how much space the water takes up. You can fit more slow-moving molecules into a space than you can fast-moving ones.

This is why bodies of water at different temperatures have different densities. Dissolving something in water can also change the water's density. Salt dissolved in water actually increases the water's weight.

Bodies of water separated by density are responsible for the currents that flow through the ocean. When water warmed at the equator expands, it begins to flow toward the poles. As the water flows toward the poles, it cools and sinks, pushing cold water out of its way. The cold water then moves toward the equator, where it is warmed. These movements have a huge effect on our climate and environment.

In this activity, you will have an opportunity to explore how waters of different densities stay separated and how they interact with one another.

Water Density

What You Need

- A pitcher
- Ice cubes
- Water
- A paper cup
- Food coloring (red and blue)
- An eyedropper
- A clear drinking glass
- Table salt
- A tablespoon
- A large baking pan

What You'll Do

#1   Fill the pitcher halfway with ice, and then add water until it is full. Allow the pitcher to stand for five minutes.

#2   Pour cold water from the pitcher into the paper cup. Add several drops of blue food coloring to the water in the cup.

#3   Fill the eyedropper with cold blue water from the cup.

Water Density

#4 Fill the clear drinking glass with warm water. Put the tip of the eyedropper into the glass of warm water. Squeeze several drops of cold blue water into the glass. What happens to the cold water?

#5 Empty the glass and refill it with cold water from the pitcher.

#6 Empty the paper cup and refill it with warm tap water. Add several drops of red food coloring to the water in the cup.

#7 Fill the eyedropper with warm red water from the cup. Put the tip of the eyedropper into the glass of cold water. Squeeze several drops of warm red water into the glass. What happens to the warm water?

#8 Empty the paper cup and add three tablespoons of table salt to it. Then add cold water to the cup and stir the water until the salt dissolves. Add three drops of blue food coloring to the water in the cup.

#9 Fill the large baking pan halfway with water. Set the pan on a table.

#10 Slowly pour the blue salt water down the inside of the baking pan into the water. What happens to the salt water?

Water Density

Analyzing Your Results

#1 Which is more dense, warm water or cold water? How can you tell?

#2 Where in the ocean would you expect to find the coldest water?

#3 Which is more dense, salt water or freshwater? Why?

For Further Investigation

#1 Over a period of time, experiment with water that is separated by temperature. The cold water will eventually become warmer, and the warm water will eventually become cooler. After some time, they will become the same temperature. Fill a jar halfway with warm water. Carefully pour cold, colored water into the jar. What happens when all of the water becomes the same temperature?

#2 In an experiment similar to the previous one, mix two bodies of water that have different amounts of salt. Do the two layers of water mix over time?

4 Pressure and Depth

When you lift a glass of water to drink from it, you will notice that the water makes the glass heavier. If you have ever carried a bucket of water, you know that water can be very heavy. Because water has weight, deeper water exerts more pressure. Pressure is the force that water makes as it presses down on an object. Objects are under pressure from the weight of the water above pushing down on them.

If you dive to the bottom of a deep swimming pool, you will probably feel pressure on your ears. Scuba divers go much deeper than the bottom of a swimming pool, but even they can swim only so deep. At the deepest point in the ocean, the pressure is more than seven tons per square inch!

In this activity, you will explore how water creates pressure. Do you know how to change the amount of water pressure on an object? Do the following experiment to find out.

Pressure and Depth

What You Need

- A 1-gallon milk jug or other large jug
- A paper cup
- A ruler
- A pencil or pen and paper
- A nail
- Masking tape
- Water

What You'll Do

#1   Use a pencil or pen to mark both the milk jug and the paper cup at 1 inch (2.5 cm) and 3 inches (7.5 cm). With the nail, punch a small hole in the milk jug and the paper cup at the 1-inch (2.5 cm) mark.

#2   Cover each hole with a piece of masking tape. Fill the milk jug and the paper cup with water to the 3-inch (7.5 cm) mark.

#3   Lay the ruler beside the paper cup. Remove the tape, and measure the farthest distance that the water shoots from the paper cup.

Pressure and Depth

#4 Lay the ruler beside the milk jug. Remove the tape, and measure the farthest distance that the water shoots from the milk jug.

#5 Use a pencil or pen to mark the milk jug at 6 inches (15 cm) and 9 inches (22.5 cm). Replace the tape, and fill the milk jug with water to the 6-inch (15 cm) mark.

#6 Place the ruler beside the milk jug. Remove the tape, and measure the farthest distance that the water shoots from the milk jug.

#7 Replace the tape, and fill the milk jug with water to the 9-inch (22.5 cm) mark. Place the ruler beside the milk jug. Remove the tape, and measure the farthest distance that the water shoots from the milk jug.

Analyzing Your Results

#1 How did the volume of the two containers affect the distance that the water traveled?

#2 Make a graph of the distance that the water shot from the milk jug. Put the height of the water in the jug on the *x-axis* (or horizontal line). Put the distance the water traveled on the *y-axis* (or vertical line).

#3 Based on your graph, how far would the water travel if the height of the water in the milk jug was 4.5 inches (11.4 cm)? Test your prediction by filling the milk jug with water to a height of 4.5 inches (11.4 cm) and measuring the water stream. Were you correct?

#4 Based on your graph, how far would the water travel if the height of the water in the milk jug was 12 inches (30 cm)?

For Further Investigation

If you have a piece of PVC pipe, you can try the following experiment: You can test the pressure of a very tall column of water. You will need an adult to help you seal the bottom of the pipe and to drill a hole in it. Then you can do the previous experiment, using the PVC pipe in place of the milk jug.

PVC pipe

5 Wave Energy

If you hold one end of a jump rope and give it a quick flick, you will see a wave pass through the rope. Waves travel through water in the same way that they pass through a jump rope. A wave may look like a mass of water moving across the surface, but it is not. When a wave passes by, very little water actually moves forward. Instead, the wave moves the water up and down, just as it moves the jump rope.

A wave is an energy pulse that goes through the water. Energy is passed from one water molecule to the next. The water is known as the medium, which is the object through which the wave moves. When energy passes through the water molecules, these molecules squeeze together. That is what gives waves their characteristic humps.

Most ocean waves are caused by wind blowing across the water. Ocean waves can be as small as tiny ripples in the sea's surface. They can also be as large as a tsunami. A tsunami is an ocean wave that can travel as fast as 600 miles per hour and can cross an entire ocean. When this kind of wave approaches the shore, it grows to an enormous size. Tsunamis can cause great damage. They can even be deadly.

Large wave

In this activity, you will see how waves work. You will watch the way energy moves from molecule to molecule. You will also discover how much the water itself moves within a wave.

What You Need

- A book
- Six marbles
- A large baking pan
- Water
- Food coloring

Wave Energy

What You'll Do

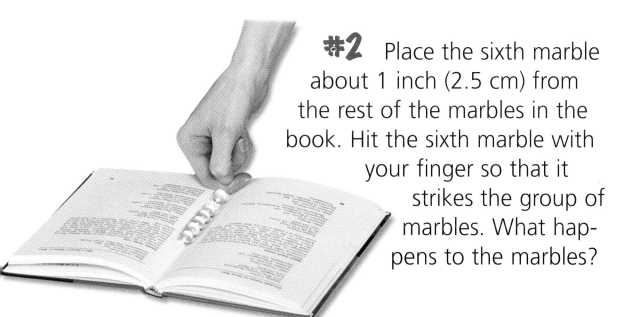

#1 Open the book and lay it flat on a table. Place five marbles in the groove in the center of the book. All five marbles should be pushed together in the middle of the book.

#2 Place the sixth marble about 1 inch (2.5 cm) from the rest of the marbles in the book. Hit the sixth marble with your finger so that it strikes the group of marbles. What happens to the marbles?

#3 Fill the baking pan with water and set it on a table.

#4 After the water has stopped moving, add one drop of food coloring to the center of the baking pan.

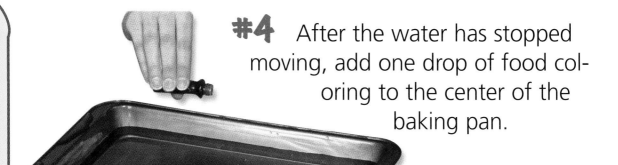

#5 Create a wave at one end of the baking pan by tapping your finger on the surface of the water. What happens to the drop of food coloring as the wave passes it?

Wave Energy

Analyzing Your Results

#1 Why did the last marble in the line move when the first marble in the line was struck?

#2 Think of the marbles as tiny molecules of water. How do you think the energy from a wave travels through water?

For Further Investigation

#1 Experiment with more and fewer marbles. Does the number of marbles in the line affect the way they move? What does this show about energy transfer?

#2 Separate the marbles in the line. How does that affect the transfer of energy from one marble to another?

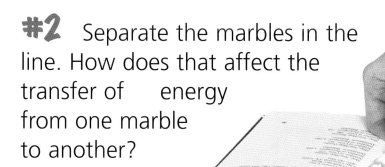

6 Tides and Shorelines

Have you ever been to the seashore? If so, you have probably noticed all the shells on the beach. How do these shells, sometimes many feet away from the water's edge, get to the shore? It is all because of the tides. The tides are the regular rise and fall of the sea level. At high tide, the water comes farthest onto the beach. At low tide, the water is at its lowest point on the beach.

Earth as seen from the moon

Tides are caused by the gravitational pull of the moon on the oceans. The moon's gravity pulls the water in the oceans toward the moon. Gravity is the force that causes objects to move toward one another.

The moon's pull is strongest on the part of the earth that faces it. In fact, the pull is so strong that it gathers the ocean water into a peak, which forms a high tide.

While this is happening, the earth is also rotating, or spinning. The rotation pushes the water away from the earth. This causes another peak to form on the side of the earth opposite the moon, which is another high tide. When the two high tides form, they pull water away from other parts of the earth. As the water drains from these areas, they experience a low tide.

Tides can change depending upon the location of the earth, sun, and moon and on the time of year. Some bodies of water, such as the Caribbean Sea, have only one high tide and one low tide each day. Others, such as the North Sea, have two high tides and two low tides each day. Some have very gentle tides, whereas others have large tides. The Bay of Fundy has the highest tides in the world. They average about 45 feet (15 m) between high and low tides. The average ocean tide is only about 2.5 feet (76 cm).

The shape and type of shoreline can affect tides as well. The shoreline is the line where a body of water and the shore meet. In this activity, you will experiment with different types of shorelines to see how tides change. If you can, do this experiment outdoors. You will be sloshing water, and you do not want to make a mess in your house!

What You Need

- A square baking pan
- A round baking pan
- A pie pan
- Water

What You'll Do

#1 Fill each pan completely with water.

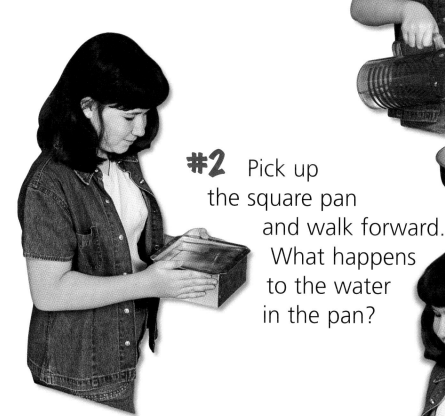

#2 Pick up the square pan and walk forward. What happens to the water in the pan?

#3 Repeat Step #2 for the round pan and the pie pan. Note any differences in the amount of water that spills out of each pan.

Experiment #6

Analyzing Your Results

#1 From which pan did the most water spill?

#2 How did the shape of that pan compare to the shapes of the other pans?

Miami Beach Coastline —a straight coastline

#3 Repeat the experiment with the square pan, but this time, hold the pan by two corners. Did more or less water spill from this pan than before? How can you explain the results?

#4 What type of coastline would you expect to have the highest and lowest tides?

Caribbean Coastline—a curved coastline

Tides and Shorelines

For Further Investigation

#1 Use modeling clay to make a coastline in the square pan. Make shorelines with gentle slopes and with bays of different sizes. How do these shorelines affect the amount of water that spills from the pan?

#2 Try holding the model coastlines perpendicular and parallel to the direction you move. How does this affect the way the water behaves? Do the tides increase or decrease?

glossary

buoyancy   The upward force that water exerts on an object.

condensation   The process through which a gas changes to a liquid.

density   The weight of a given volume of water.

evaporation   The process through which a liquid changes to a gas.

gravity   The force that causes objects to move toward one another.

molecules   Tiny particles that make up all matter.

precipitation   Rain, sleet, snow, or hail that falls to the earth.

pressure   The force water makes as it presses down on an object.

shoreline   The line where a body of water and the shore meet.

tide   The regular rise and fall of the sea level.

volume   The amount of space that an object takes up.

water cycle   The process through which water moves between the ocean, air, and land; sometimes called the hydrologic cycle.

wave   A movement in a medium by which energy is transferred from one molecule to another.

These Web sites will help you find out more about oceans.

Ace on the Case: Secrets@Sea

http://www.secretsatsea.org/

Cool Science for Curious Kids

http://www.hhmi.org/coolscience

Cyberspace Middle School—Science Fair Projects

http://www.scri.fsu.edu/~dennisl/special/sf_projects.html

The Evergreen Project, Inc.

http://www.mobot.org/MBGnet/salt/oceans/index.htm

Exploratorium

http://www.exploratorium.edu

Newton Ask a Scientist

http://newton.dep.anl.gov/aasquest.htm

OceanLink

http://oceanlink.island.net/

Oceans Alive

http://www.abc.net.au/oceans/alive.htm

Scientific American Explore!

http://www.sciam.com/explorations

for further reading

Barlowe, Sy. *101 Questions About the Seashore*. Mineola, NY: Dover, 1998.

Clarke, Penny. *Beneath the Oceans*. Danbury, CT: Franklin Watts, 1997.

Fredericks, Anthony D. *Exploring the Ocean: Science Activities for Kids*. Golden, CO: Fulcrum, 1998.

MacQuitty, Miranda. *Ocean*. New York: Knopf, 1995.

Nye, Bill. *Bill Nye's Consider the Ocean*. New York: Hyperion, 1998.

Ricciuti, Edward R. *Ocean*. Tarrytown, NY: Benchmark, 1995.

VanCleave, Janice P. *Janice VanCleave's Oceans for Every Kid: Easy Activities That Make Learning Science Fun*. New York: John Wiley & Sons, 1996.

index

credits

About the Author

Allan Cobb is a freelance science writer living in central Texas. He has written books, radio scripts, articles, and educational materials concerning different aspects of science. When not writing about science, he enjoys traveling, camping, hiking, and exploring caves.

Photo Credits

Cover photos by Scott Bauer. P. 13 © Buddy Mays/ International Stock; p. 17 © CORBIS/Craig Aurness; pp. 31 & 42 © SuperStock. All other photos by Scott Bauer.

Design and Layout

Laura Murawski

Series Editor

Amy Haugesag

Metric Conversions

To convert measurements in U.S. units into metric units, use the following formulas:

1 inch = 2.54 centimeters (cm)	1 ounce = 28.35 grams (g)
1 foot = 0.30 meters (m)	1 gallon = 3.79 liters (l)
1 mile = 1.609 kilometers (km)	1 pound = 453.59 grams (g)